The Children's Picture Prehistory
DINOSAURS

Anne McCord
Illustrated by Bob Hersey
Designed by Graham Round

Series Editor Lisa Watts
Consultant Editor Dr L. B. Halstead

Contents

Anne McCord is a lecturer in the Education
Section of the British Museum (Natural History).
Dr L. B. Halstead is Reader in Geology and
Zoology at the University of Reading, England.

First published in 1977 by
Usborne Publishing Ltd
20 Garrick Street
London WC2E 9BJ

© 1977 Usborne
Publishing Ltd

Printed in Belgium

The name Usborne and the device are Trade Marks of Usborne Publishing Ltd.

KT-435-698

What is Prehistory?

Iguanodon

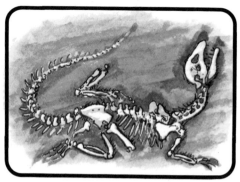

About 150 million years ago, strange creatures called dinosaurs lived on Earth. People did not exist then, but we know about dinosaurs because we have found their bones buried in the rocks.

The remains of animals and plants which lived millions of years ago are called fossils. Scientists study them to find out the story of the Earth before people wrote down history. This story is called prehistory.

It is a very long story because the Earth is about 4,600 million years old. We have made a time dial to help you follow the story of how the Earth and life began. Below, you can find out how to make a time dial of your own.

Make a time dial

You need some card, tracing paper, a paper fastener, paints, and scissors.

1 This big circle is the pattern for your time dial. Trace it on to the card. Make sure you mark the centre and all the rectangles.

2 Then trace the circle again. This time trace only the centre and the two red rectangles.

3 Cut out the circles, leaving a small tab on the one with all the rectangles. On the other circle, cut out the two red rectangles to make little windows.

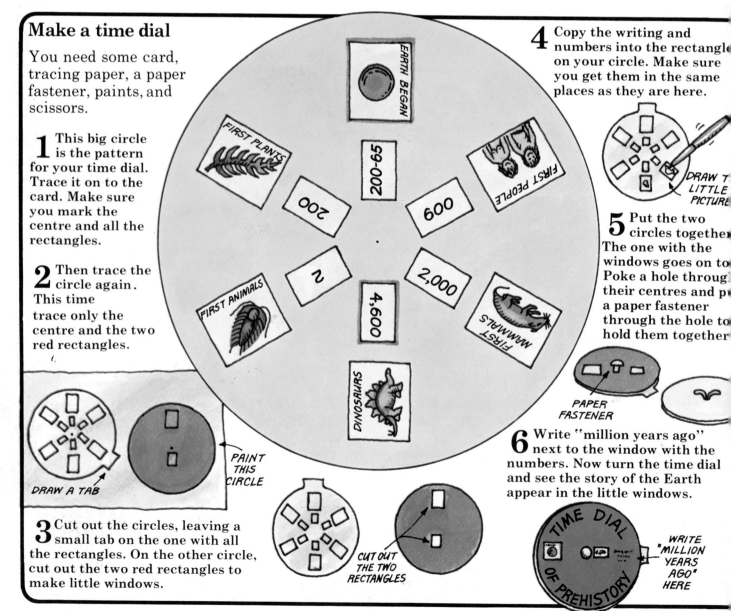

EARTH BEGAN

FIRST PLANTS

200-65

200

600

FIRST PEOPLE

2

4,600

2,000

FIRST MAMMALS

FIRST ANIMALS

DINOSAURS

DRAW A TAB

PAINT THIS CIRCLE

CUT OUT THE TWO RECTANGLES

4 Copy the writing and numbers into the rectangles on your circle. Make sure you get them in the same places as they are here.

DRAW T LITTLE PICTURE

5 Put the two circles together. The one with the windows goes on to Poke a hole throug their centres and p a paper fastener through the hole to hold them together

PAPER FASTENER

6 Write "million years ago" next to the window with the numbers. Now turn the time dial and see the story of the Earth appear in the little windows.

TIME DIAL OF PREHISTORY

WRITE "MILLION YEARS AGO" HERE

How the Earth Began

Scientists have studied the Sun, the stars and the rocks of the Earth to find out how the Earth formed. They think that about 4,700 million years ago the Earth did not exist. There was only an enormous cloud of dust and gases swirling round the Sun. Then the cloud split up to form several small clouds. Each of these probably became one of the planets which now go round the Sun.

1 — 4,600 MILLION YEARS AGO

The cloud which made the planet Earth began to shrink and became very hot. As it heated up it changed into a ball of liquid rock spinning in space.

2 — 4,000 MILLION YEARS AGO

Slowly, over millions of years, the ball of rock cooled down. A crust of solid rock hardened on the outside, but underneath the rock was still hot and liquid.

3 — 3,500 MILLION YEARS AGO

Thick clouds surrounded the Earth. When these cooled rain began to fall. It rained for thousands of years and the rain-water made rivers and oceans.

How life began

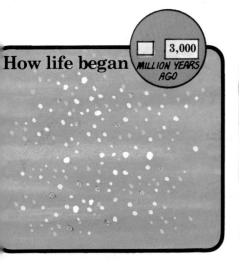

3,000 MILLION YEARS AGO

The first living things grew in the sea. They were neither animals nor plants. Scientists know very little about them because they were so tiny.

2,000 MILLION YEARS AGO

Very slowly, these tiny living things changed and became plants growing in the sea. There were no animals yet because there was no oxygen for them to breathe.

600 MILLION YEARS AGO

Plants make oxygen as they grow. Eventually there was enough oxygen for animals to grow in the sea. Some of the first animals were jellyfish and sponges like these.

The Fossil Clues

People who study the plants and animals which lived millions of years ago are called palaeontologists. They study fossils, which are all that remain of prehistoric life. A fossil is made when the remains of animals or plants slowly change to stone.

When scientists discover a plant or animal, they give it a Latin or Greek name so that people who speak different languages can use the same names. There is a list of what the names mean in English on the last page of this book.

How fossils are made

Fossils are made at the same time as the rock they are found in. Here is how it happens.

Palaeontologists travel all over the world looking for fossils. When they find them they dig them out of the rock and take them back to the laboratory.

Then they study the fossil to find out what sort of plant or animal i was. Here they are measuring a giant ammonite which lived in the sea 150 million years ago.

1

Rain and rivers wear away rocks and wash sand and mud into the sea. The sand and mud is called sediment. It slowly builds up to form thick layers on the sea floor.

2

When sea creatures die their soft bodies rot away and their shells are buried in the sediment. After millions of years the layers of sediment are very deep and heavy.

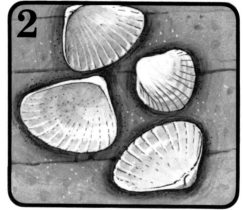

3

The sediment at the bottom is pressed down so hard that it becomes rock called sedimentary rock. The shells leave a print of their shape in the rock.

4

These prints made by shells are called fossils. Fossil prints of leaves and footprints are made like this too. Fossils of bones are made in a different way.

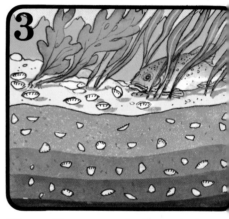

5

Bones buried in the sand are slowly dissolved away. The space left is filled by tiny grains of sand which harden into a fossil shaped like the animal's bones.

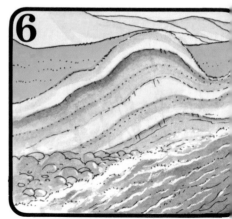

6

Movements in the Earth's crust lift the rocks above the sea. As the rocks wear away the fossils of plants and animals which lived long ago, appear on the surface.

Plants and animals in the rock

Here are the fossil remains of some plants and animals. They have not been drawn to scale. In this book the names of individual plants or animals are printed in *italics* and the names of groups of plants or animals are in ordinary type.

This is the fossil of *Seymouria,* one of the first land animals which lived 250 million years ago.

60 cm long

A birch leaf fell from its tree into a lake 30 million years ago and made this fossil print.

The fossil plant on the left is called *Neuropteris*. It grew 280 million years ago.

The tiny pits in the rock on the right were made millions of years ago by raindrops. The rain splashed on soft mud which hardened to form rock.

On the left is a fossil called a belemnite. It was part of the body of a sea creature which lived 150 million years ago.

about 4 cm long

Even the fragile wings of this *Prodryas* butterfly were fossilized when it died 40 million years ago.

Model fossils

You will need plaster of Paris, plasticine, thin card and some leaves.

Make a flat piece of plasticine, large enough to put the leaf on. Then make a ring of card to fit round the leaf.

Press the edge of the ring into the plasticine and put the leaf inside the ring. Press the leaf gently to make it lie flat.

Mix a thin paste of plaster of Paris and pour it over the leaf. Then leave it to set.

When the plaster is hard, take off the ring and peel away the plasticine. Gently pull the leaf off the plaster. Try making model fossils of sea-shells too.

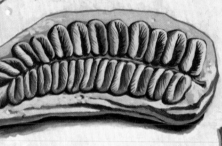

The First Life

The land was dry and lifeless 550 million years ago. But the seas and lakes were full of plants and animals like these. Scientists have worked out what they looked like from their fossils. Trilobites died out millions of years ago, but sponges, sea lilies and jellyfish still live in the sea.

Fossils of plants and animals which lived together at the same time are found in the same place in the rock. Scientists can tell what the weather was like by looking at the kind of plants that grew. Here is what they think life in the sea looked like, about 550 million years ago.

Sponges are animals and they still live in the sea today. Their soft, fleshy bodies did not make good fossils.

This is an annelid worm. There are fossils of the trails and burrows these worms made in the sand.

Trilobites crawled on the sand, looking for food. Most were between 2 and 10 cm long, but some giant trilobites were 70 cm.

Fossils of trails made by trilobites have been found in the rocks.

Reading rocks

Fossils are the same age as the sedimentary rock in which they are found. Scientists can work out how old the rocks are, so they know the age of the fossils too.

Sedimentary rock is made in layers. The layer of rock at the bottom formed first and so is the oldest. The fossils found there are older than those higher up.

1 Make some trilobites

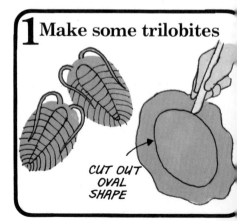

CUT OUT OVAL SHAPE

To make a model trilobite, roll out a piece of plasticine. Then cut a flat pear-shaped piece for the trilobite's body.

There were no plants or animals on the bare rocky land.

Jellyfish like these still live in the sea and catch food with their tentacles.

Sea lilies are animals, not flowers. They catch food with their wavy arms.

These are called lamp shells because they look like a kind of ancient Roman lamp.

The name trilobite means "three-lobed" and describes the shape of its body.

1 Fossil trilobites

Trilobites made good fossils because they had hard skin. Their antennae did not become fossils, but marks show where they joined the body.

Fossil jellyfish

Jellyfish did not make good fossils because their bodies were too soft. This one left a print of the shape of its body in soft mud.

2

The trilobite's hard skin protected it from danger. Some trilobites could curl into a tight ball to protect themselves.

2

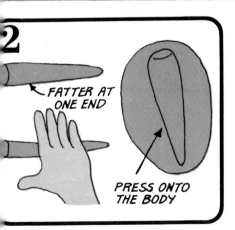

FATTER AT ONE END

PRESS ONTO THE BODY

ext, roll a sausage of plasticine e same length as the oval. One d should be a bit fatter than the her. Press this along the centre f the body.

3 PRESS ANTENNAE ONTO BODY

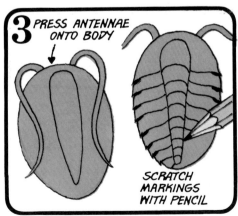

SCRATCH MARKINGS WITH PENCIL

Roll a long, thin sausage shape and cut it in half to make two antennae. Then scratch the markings on the trilobite with the point of a pencil.

4 LEAVES STUCK IN PLASTICINE   CARROT TOPS

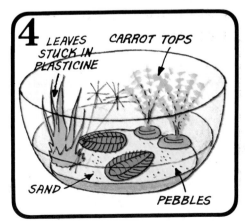

SAND   PEBBLES

You could make an underwater scene by putting the trilobites on some sand in a bowl. To make plants cut off the tops of carrots and put them in water to sprout.

The First Fish

For millions of years the seas stayed warm and calm. Trilobites still crawled over the sea floor, but there were new creatures too. Some had shells and others lived in a chalky skeleton of coral. All these animals are called invertebrates because they had no backbones.

As time passed, some animals developed backbones and became fish. Animals with backbones are called vertebrates. The way animals slowly change, is called evolution. This is explained on page 13.

1 Life in the sea

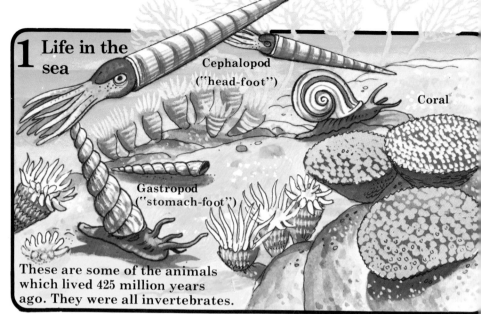

Cephalopod ("head-foot")

Coral

Gastropod ("stomach-foot")

These are some of the animals which lived 425 million years ago. They were all invertebrates.

2

about 1 m long

The first animals with backbones were fish-like creatures called ostracoderms. They had thick, armoured skin and their name means "shell-skinned".

3

Acanthodii fish, about 10 cm long

The first fish were jawless but later fish had jaws with sharp teeth. They could swim very fast to catch other sea creatures and eat them.

Plants on land

Plants first grew on the land 400 million years ago. They grew on wet, marshy ground near water. Then stronger plants grew and spread over the rest of the land.

The great drought

About 375 million years ago the weather became very hot. There were long seasons of drought and the lakes and rivers dried up in the hot sun.

Many fish died as the lakes shrank. Their bodies lay on the sun-baked mud and sand blew over them. It was so dry that their bodies did not rot away.

Fossil fish

This is the fossil of a group of fish which died when the lakes dried up. Their bodies were so well preserved that the fossils show the shape of their scales.

Prehistoric sea monster

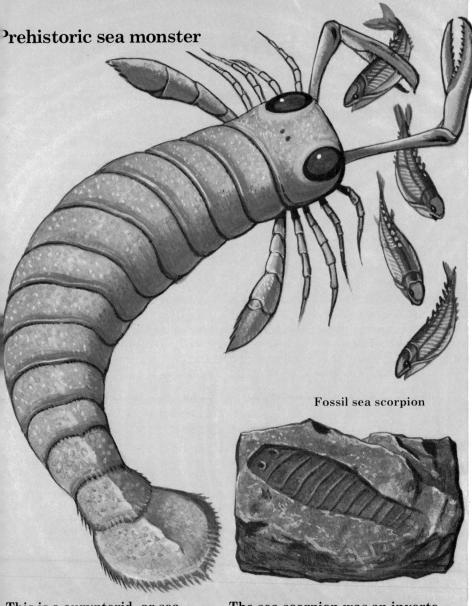

Fossil sea scorpion

This is a eurypterid, or sea scorpion, which lived 400 million years ago. It was about 3 m long and caught small creatures with its long pincers.

The sea scorpion was an invertebrate and so had no backbone. It had a hard skin which was jointed so that it could move. On this fossil you can see the marks of its eyes.

Fish on land

This is a fish called *Eusthenopteron*. It survived the drought because it was able to drag itself across the land to find a pool or stream. It was about 50 cm long.

Eusthenopteron had a lung as well as gills, so it could breathe on land. It had strong bones in its fins which it used to pull itself along the ground.

Make a sea scorpion

Here is how to make a wriggly cardboard model of a sea scorpion.

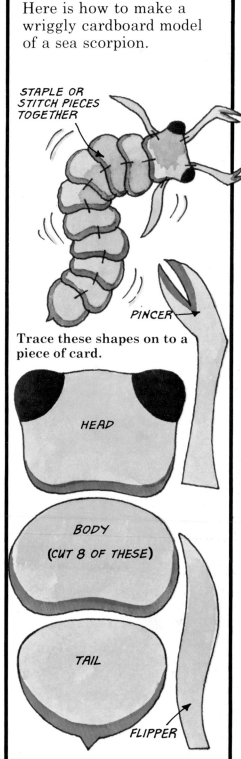

STAPLE OR STITCH PIECES TOGETHER

PINCER

Trace these shapes on to a piece of card.

HEAD

BODY (CUT 8 OF THESE)

TAIL

FLIPPER

Paint the shapes and then cut them out of the card. Take one of the body pieces and staple or stitch it to the head. Then join on the rest of the pieces and put the tail on the end. Staple the flippers to the side of the head and put the pincers on the front. To make the scorpion wriggle, twitch its tail.

Animals Crawl on to Land

The first creatures to survive on land were fish with lungs and strong fins. Over the next few million years they slowly changed and became more suited to living on the land. Their fins became legs which were strong enough for walking and their lungs grew bigger.

Animals which live on land but have to return to the water to lay their eggs are called amphibians. The first land animals on Earth were amphibians. The weather was hot and rainy then and there were plenty of pools where they could lay their eggs.

The first amphibian

One of the first amphibians was *Ichthyostega*. It was about 1 m long and lived 345 million years ago. It had strong legs and feet with five toes, but its tail was like that of a fish.

Its legs were strong enough to carry it on land, but it probably stayed most of the time in the water, swimming and catching fish to eat.

Did you know?

Insects

Meganeura

The first insects lived at this time too. This is the fossil of *Meganeura*, an insect which looked like a huge dragonfly. It lived near swamps and ate other insects.

Cockroach fossil

This is the fossil of a cockroach which lived at the same time as the amphibians. Cockroaches, and other insects were probably eaten by the amphibians.

The life of amphibians

The modern frog is an amphibian. The adult frog lives on land and its life-cycle is the same as that of the first amphibians.

Frogs have to lay their eggs in water. The eggs have no shells and would dry up if they were laid on the land.

The eggs hatch into tadpoles which swim in the water with their tails. They breathe through gills and eat plants.

As the tadpoles grow, th tails and gills disappear. They grow into adult fro with legs and lungs and move onto the land.

rehistoric forests

hick forests covered the land
bout 300 million years ago. In
ne forests there were lakes and
wamps full of rotting leaves
nd plants.

Giant clubmosses grew
30 m tall with trunks
nearly a metre across.
Scars on the trunks were
left by leaves which had
dropped off.

Meganeura

This is the trunk of
Calamites, a kind of
horsetail which grew
18 m tall.

Amphibians lived near
lakes and swamps in the
forest and ate fish or
insects.

Cockroaches ate the
leaves and rotting
plants.

Horsetails like these still
grow in marshy places
today.

Mosses, ferns and
liverworts grew on
the wet ground.

1 How coal is made

2

3

oal is made from plants which
rew 300 million years ago. Dead
ranches and leaves fell into the
wamps. Slowly they built up into
thick layer of rotting plants.

Later the swamps were covered by
the sea. The rotting wood and
leaves were buried under thick
layers of mud and sand at the
bottom of the sea.

The heavy layers of sand and mud
squashed the plants and changed
them into coal. Now we dig
through the ground to reach the
coal and burn it to make heat.

The First Reptiles

About 280 million years ago the weather changed again and became very hot and dry. The swamps slowly dried up and most of the amphibians died.

Now a new kind of animal evolved. It had thick, scaly skin and laid eggs which were protected by a leathery shell. This type of animal is called a reptile.

The new reptiles laid their eggs in the warm sand or in nests of rotting plants. The shell protected them from drying up in the hot sun.

Diadectes was one of the earliest reptiles. It measured about 2 m from its nose to the end of its long tail. Fossils of its teeth show that it ate plants.

Its legs stuck out on either side of its body and so did not support it very well. But they were strong enough to lift its body off the ground and take quite long steps.

Land animals of 200 million years ago

Gradually, over millions of years, some of the reptiles changed. They had different teeth, their legs were stronger and some of them had hair instead of scales. Animals which have hair and suckle their young are called mammals. Parts of some of the reptiles' bodies were like mammals and these are called mammal-like reptiles.

Lystrosaurus was a mammal-like reptile, which lived in swamps and ate plants. It was about 1½ m long.

Sauroctonus was a fierce mammal-like reptile. It had long, sharp teeth and ate other animals.

Euparkeria was a reptile which lived about 225 million years ago. It was about 1 m long and was the ancestor of some of the dinosaurs.

Thrinaxodon was a mammal-like reptile which had developed hair, but it probably still laid eggs. It was about the size of a cat.

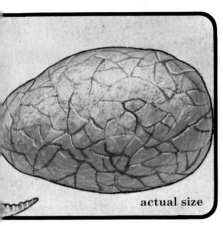

actual size

is fossil egg is about 225 million
ars old. We do not know which
ptile laid it but we can see that
e tough shell dried and cracked
fore it became a fossil.

Edaphosaurus was a reptile which
lived 250 million years ago. It
was about 3 m long. The strange
sail on its back was made of
long bones covered with skin.

It may have used the sail to keep
its body at the right temperature.
When it was cold it heated up
quickly by turning the sail to the
heat of the sun.

What is a reptile?

Reptiles are animals which
have scaly skin and lay eggs
with shells. They are cold-
blooded, which means they
cannot control the
temperature of their body.

What is evolution?

The way animals slowly
change, over millions of
years, and become new kinds
of animals, is called
evolution. The first person to
discover how animals evolve
was a scientist called Charles
Darwin, who lived over a
hundred years ago.

Darwin showed that no two
animals are exactly the same,
even among the same type of
animal. Some of them are
taller, or stronger, or have
other features which may

make them more suited to
living in their surroundings.

The animals which are
better adapted survive to
become adults and have
babies like themselves.
Eventually, after many
generations of babies, the
animals which are less well
adapted have all died out.
This is called the "survival of
the fittest" and it explains
how a group of animals
evolves and becomes well
suited to its surroundings.

1

About 375 million years ago the
weather changed and there were
long, dry seasons. One kind of
fish, called *Eusthenopteron*, was

2

able to survive because it had
strong fins and could drag itself
across the land to find pools.
Many of the other fish died.

3

Over the next few million
years, some of the descendants
of *Eusthenopteron* were born with
even stronger fins.

4

Eventually, about 345 million
years ago, some animals had
legs and these were the first
amphibians.

The Age of Dinosaurs

Dinosaurs were a group of reptiles which lived from 200 million years to 65 million years ago. Palaeontologists have found thousands of fossils which show what dinosaurs looked like and how they lived. There are fossils of bones and teeth, footprints and skin and even fossil eggs with baby dinosaurs inside.

The name dinosaur means "terrible lizard". There were dinosaurs on the Earth for about 135 million years, which is 70 times longer than people have existed.

The first dinosaurs

Coelophysis

Fabrosaurus

These are two of the earliest dinosaurs. *Fabrosaurus* was about 1 m long. It ate plants and usually walked on four legs, but could run faster on two.

The other dinosaur, *Coelophysis* was about 2 m long. It walked on two legs and had a long tail to help it balance. It had sharp teeth and ate meat.

Dinosaur timetable

There were lots of different kinds of dinosaurs, but they did not all live at the same time. This chart shows you when some of the main kinds of dinosaurs lived.

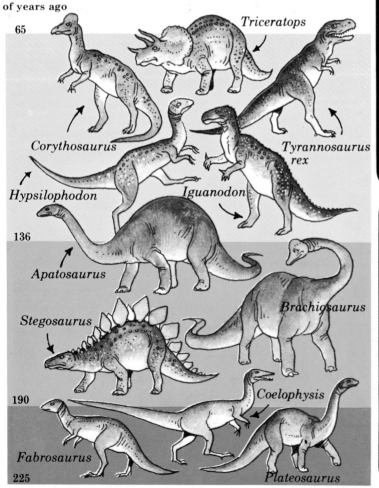

Millions of of years ago

65

Triceratops

Corythosaurus

Tyrannosaurus rex

Hypsilophodon

Iguanodon

136

Apatosaurus

Stegosaurus

Brachiosaurus

190

Coelophysis

Fabrosaurus

225

Plateosaurus

Prehistoric footprints

Fossil footprints of *Megalosaurus*, a huge meat-eating dinosaur, show the shape of its three toes. The footprints were made when it walked on soft mud. The mud was baked by the sun and later covered by sand. This hardened to form rock which still had the shape of the footprints in it.

Fossil skin

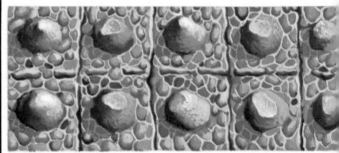

This is a piece of fossil skin from the dinosaur *Scolosaurus*. This dinosaur had thick, scaly skin with spikes to protect it.

You can see the shape of the scales and the bony spikes. The fossil is stone-coloured and does not show the real colour of the skin.

Dinosaurs' ancestors

Millerosaurus

30 cm long

Shansisuchus
2 m long

Saltoposuchus
120 cm long

The ancestors of the dinosaurs were reptiles like *Millerosaurus* which lived 250 million years ago. They crawled on the ground with their legs stuck out at their sides.

Shansisuchus was a reptile which lived 225 million years ago. Its legs were tucked under its body and lifted it well off the ground, although it was a heavy animal.

Saltoposuchus was the ancestor of some of the two-legged dinosaurs. Dinosaurs had stronger legs than the early reptiles and had long tails to help them balance.

Baby dinosaurs

Baby dinosaurs hatched from eggs which the mother dinosaur laid in the sand.

Fossil eggs of the dinosaur *Protoceratops* have been found with the bones of the baby dinosaurs inside. The young looked just like the adult dinosaurs. *Protoceratops* was a ceratopsian dinosaur, about

2 m long.

The mother *Protoceratops* dug a nest in the sand and laid her eggs in it. But she did not look after them. Eggs were sometimes buried in sand and the babies died.

Monster quiz

We have mixed up the letters in these reptiles' names. Can you work out what the names ought to be be? The answers are on the last page of this book.

1 Donoguani—This one had spikes on its thumbs.

2 Pertosaurs—These were flying reptiles.

3 Gosetsaurus—This dinosaur had spikes on its tail.

4 Rantynosaurus—A very fierce dinosaur.

5 Chabriosaurus—The biggest and heaviest dinosaur.

6 Harodsaurs—These dinosaurs had bony crests on their heads.

Finding Dinosaur Fossils

Fossils form in sedimentary rocks, so palaeontologists know where to look for them. When they go to a place where there are sedimentary rocks they will probably find fossils.

The most exciting thing to find is a dinosaur fossil. It may be a dinosaur that is already known, but they might find a new kind of dinosaur that no-one has found before.

Once they have found the fossil bones it may take several years to put them together and work out what the dinosaur looked like.

If the skeleton has fallen apart, the palaeontologists note where each bone is lying. This helps them when they try to put the skeleton together again.

The fossil bones are very fragile. They have to be wrapped in wet tissue and then covered with strips of cloth dipped in plaster of Paris to protect them.

Making mistakes

Sometimes scientists make mistakes when they reconstruct dinosaurs. When they first discovered *Iguanodon*, they thought it had a horn on its nose.

Later they realised that *Iguanodon* had no horn but a spike on each of its thumbs. Now scientists know more about dinosaurs and make fewer mistakes.

Fossil skeleton

The picture below shows the fossil skeleton of the dinosaur *Plateosaurus*. On the right you can see what palaeontologists think *Plateosaurus* looked like when it was alive.

In museums, you can sometimes see wires holding the skeleton in a life-like pose. If it is a very rare fossil, fibre-glass models of the bones are shown instead of the real fossil bones.

When palaeontologists have cleaned all the fossil bones they fit them together to make the skeleton. Broken bones have to be stuck together, rather like a jig-saw puzzle. If any of the bones are missing they have to use bones from another dinosaur of the same type.

3

metimes the fossil is almost
mpletely buried in solid rock.
en the whole block of rock has
be cut out and taken back to
e laboratory.

he living dinosaur

ateosaurus ("flat lizard") was
out 6 m long. It was one of the
st plant-eating dinosaurs and
ed about 200 million years ago.

ues on the fossil bones help
laeontologists reconstruct
at a living dinosaur looked
e. All animals' bones have
mps and scars which show where
e muscles joined them. By
udying the lumps on the fossil
nes, scientists can work out
e shape of the dinosaur's
uscles.

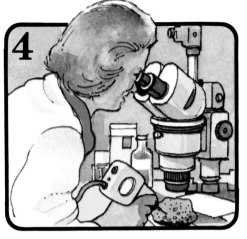

4

The rock round the fossil is
removed with tiny drills, or
washed away with chemicals. The
palaeontologist has to be very
careful not to damage the fossil.

Fossils of dinosaur skin
show that they had thick,
scaly skin, like a modern
crocodile's. There are no
fossils to show us what
colour they were. Many
large, modern reptiles are
greeny-brown, so perhaps
dinosaurs were the same.

Pipecleanosaurus

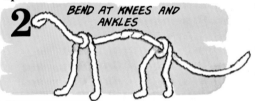

We have called our model
dinosaur Pipecleanosaurus
because it is made of
pipe-cleaners.

1 TWIST ENDS TOGETHER

PIPE CLEANERS

To make Pipecleanosaurus, join
two pipe-cleaners by twisting the
ends together. Then bend them to
make the curve of the dinosaur's
spine.

2 BEND AT KNEES AND ANKLES

Bend two pipe-cleaners in half for
the legs. Twist them round the
spine as shown in the picture.
Then bend them at the knees and
ankles.

3 LONGEST RIB IN THE MIDDLE

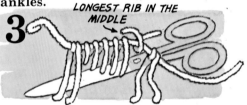

To make ribs, cut one piece of
pipe-cleaner 8 cm long, two 7 cm,
two 6 cm and two 5 cm long. Then
twist them round the spine.

4 CURVE RIBS INWARDS

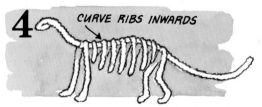

Now bend the ribs to curve them
inwards slightly. You could make
models of other skeletons in this
book too.

What Dinosaurs Ate

Some dinosaurs ate plants and others were meat-eaters. The giant dinosaurs, such as *Brachiosaurus,* ate only plants and must have eaten nearly a tonne of leaves every day to stay alive. Animals which eat plants are called herbivores and meat-eating animals are called carnivores.

Carnivorous dinosaurs had long, sharp claws for attacking their prey and pointed teeth for tearing the meat. The herbivores had to defend themselves from the fierce carnivores.

Plant-eating dinosaurs

Camarasaurus

Scolosaurus ("thorn lizard") about 6 m long

The herbivores were not all competing for the same food. The giant dinosaurs could reach the leaves in the treetops and small dinosaurs ate plants on the ground.

Fighting off the meat-eaters

Some herbivores lived together in packs to defend themselves from carnivores. Here are some of the other ways they defended themselves.

Polacanthus had thick scaly skin with spikes on its back and bony plates on its tail. Its name means "many spined".

about 5 m long

Hypsilophodon was a small dinosaur about 60 cm long. It had long legs and could run fast to escape.

Deinonychus was a carnivore. It had huge claws with which it held and killed its prey.

about 10 m long

about 5 m long

Stegosaurus had large, bony plates growing from the skin on its back and spikes like daggers on its tail. Its plates are like roof tiles and its name means "roof-lizard".

This herbivore is called *Euoplocephalus*. It stunned its attackers with the bony club on its tail. It measured 5 m from nose to tail.

Iguanodon was about 5 m tall.

A fierce carnivore

Tyrannosaurus rex was the largest carnivore. Its name means "king of the tyrant reptiles". It weighed over eight tonnes and was nearly 15 m long. Most carnivores moved on their hind legs and could run fast to catch their prey. *Tyrannosaurus rex* had very short front arms. Here, it is attacking a sauropod dinosaur called *Alamosaurus*.

einonychus was m long and the name eans "terrible claw".

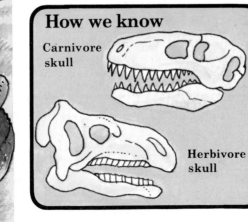

How we know

Carnivore skull

Herbivore skull

We can tell what dinosaurs ate by looking at their teeth. Carnivores had long, sharp teeth, but the herbivores' teeth were flat for chewing tough plants.

Dinosaur dropping

Fossils of dinosaur droppings are called coprolites. Scientists can tell what the dinosaurs ate by grinding the coprolites and examining the dust.

19

The Giant Dinosaurs

The giant dinosaurs are the largest land animals that have ever lived. They ate only plants and spent much of the time in swamps, where they were safe from the meat-eating dinosaurs. They belong to a group called the sauropod dinosaurs.

1 How they moved

These dinosaurs lived in swamps. It was easier for them to move in the water than on dry land.

2

They had thick, pillar-like legs to support the weight of their huge bodies.

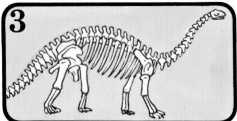

3

The bones in their legs were very strong, but their spines were hollow to make them lighter.

4

In deep water they pushed themselves along with their front legs and steered with their tails.

The heaviest dinosaur

Brachiosaurus is the largest dinosaur that has ever been discovered. It was 25 m long, 12 m high and must have weighed about 81 tonnes. It had a very long neck and could reach for leaves in the top of trees. Its name means "arm-lizard".

In herds for safety

Apatosaurus used to be called Brontosaurus. These dinosaurs stayed together in herds to protect themselves from attack by the meat-eating dinosaurs.

The longest dinosaur

Diplodocus measured 28 m from its nose to the tip of its tail. It lived in the swamps and came on land to eat plants and leaves and to lay its eggs.

The brain of *Diplodocus* was no bigger than a hen's egg. It had another nerve centre between its legs which controlled its back legs and tail.

Nostril

The sauropod dinosaurs all had very small heads. Their nostrils were on top of their heads so they could breathe when they were swimming.

Why were they so big?

Dinosaurs were probably cold-blooded. This means that their body temperature was controlled by the heat of the sun. If the weather was cool, the dinosaurs

got cold. But some of the dinosaurs were so big that it took them a very long time to cool. Their great size kept them warm and this was probably one of the reasons they were so big.

Apatosaurus means "deceptive lizard". It was about 18 m long, nearly as long as a railway carriage, and weighed about 30 tonnes. Compared to the size of its body, it had a smaller brain than any other animal.

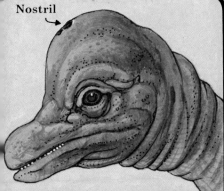

Measure some dinosaurs

1 METRE

To see how big some of the dinosaurs were, pace out their lengths in a park or play-ground. Your pace is probably about 1 m long. (If you want to be exact you can measure it.) To measure *Diplodocus*, which was 28 m long, mark where you start and take 28 paces. Then look back and see just how huge it really was.

Smallest dinosaur

Compsognathus was the smallest dinosaur. It was about the size of a crow. It fed on insects and small reptiles and could run very fast.

Horned and Crested Dinosaurs

Some dinosaurs had strange crests of bone on their heads. These belonged to a group called the hadrosaurs. The crest probably worked as a very sensitive nose which helped the hadrosaurs smell enemies from far away.

Another group of dinosaurs had horns on their heads and bony shields round their necks. These were the ceratopsians.

Hadrosaurs and ceratopsians were plant-eating dinosaurs. They probably developed their special heads to protect them from the carnivores.

Duck-billed dinosaurs

9 m long

Corythosaurus was a hadrosaur with a crest shaped like a helmet. The crest was made of bone with air tubes inside which led to the animal's lungs.

The hadrosaurs are also called duck-billed dinosaurs, because their jaws ended in a horny, toothless beak. They used this to clip leaves from the trees.

Horned dinosaurs

11 m long

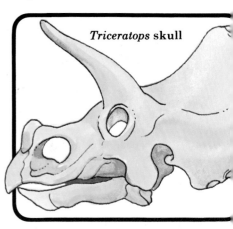

Triceratops skull

Triceratops was one of the ceratopsian dinosaurs. It had three horns, one on its nose and one over each eye. Round its neck it had a long shield of bone.

At the end of its mouth it had a beak to chop through the stems of plants. It ate very tough leaves and had special teeth with flat surfaces to chew through them.

This is the skull of *Triceratops*. Ceratopsian dinosaurs had strong jaw muscles to help them chew tough plants. The bony neck shield supported these jaw muscles.

Bone-heads

9 m long

The bone-headed dinosaurs had thick skulls with solid bone about 20 cm thick on top. This probably protected them when they fought.

These dinosaurs lived together in herds. The males may have fought each other to prove which of them was the strongest.

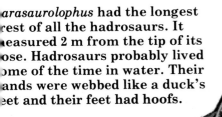

arasaurolophus had the longest rest of all the hadrosaurs. It easured 2 m from the tip of its ose. Hadrosaurs probably lived ome of the time in water. Their ands were webbed like a duck's eet and their feet had hoofs.

about 12 m long

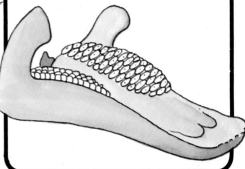

Hadrosaur teeth

Hadrosaurs had rows of hundreds of small, sharp teeth in their jaws. They ate tough pine needles and when their teeth wore down, new ones grew to replace them.

Shadow monsters

Can you recognise these reptiles from their shadows? They are all shown in this book, so look through the pages if you get stuck.

1
2   3
4
5   6
7
8
9
10   11

(Answers on the last page of this book)

Sea Monsters

At the same time as dinosaurs lived there were huge creatures living in the sea. They evolved from reptiles which lived on the land 280 million years ago. Over millions of years their bodies became smooth and streamlined to suit their life in the sea and their legs became flippers.

These sea creatures were reptiles, but they did not lay eggs. There are fossils of sea reptiles with babies inside them and these show that they gave birth to live young. This picture shows three different kinds of sea reptile.

A famous fossil find

Mary Anning lived in Dorset about 150 years ago, in a small village by the sea. She used to go fossil hunting along the beach with her father.

They found lots of fossils of ammonites and when she was 11 she found a nearly perfect fossil of an ichthyosaur.

She was the first person to discover a complete plesiosaur fossil. Her fossils are now in the Natural History Museum, London.

Ichthyosaurs were very fast swimmers. They had strong tail fins and could probably leap out of the water. Their long jaws were full of sharp teeth and they ate fish and shellfish. There were lots of different kinds of ichthyosaur which means "fish lizard" and some were about 12 m long.

Pliosaurs had short necks and large heads with lots of sharp teeth. They had strong flippers and could dive deep into the water to catch fish and ammonites.

Fossil ichthyosaur

This fossil of an ichthyosaur is so well preserved that we can see the outline of its skin. It had very large eyes so that it could see in the dark water.

It used its strong tail fin for swimming and steered with the fins on its sides. The fin on its bac stopped its body rolling from side to side as it swam.

Fossil teeth marks

This is the fossil shell of an ammonite, a sea creature which lived at the same time as the sea reptiles. This one has marks of a sea reptile's teeth on it.

Plesiosaurs had very long necks. They pulled themselves through the water with large, flat flippers and could swing their heads from side to side looking for fish. Some were about 12 m long.

Plesiosaur skeleton

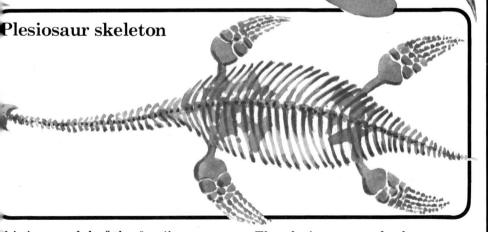

This is a model of the fossil skeleton of a plesiosaur. These sea reptiles had small skulls and some of them had as many as 76 bones in their long necks.

The plesiosaurs and other sea reptiles evolved from land animals. Their leg bones changed shape and became paddles for swimming in the water.

Felt pliosaur

You will need some felt, dried lentils or rice, tracing paper and two small buttons.

1 Fold the tracing paper. Put the fold on the edge of the pattern and trace it.

2 Keep the paper folded and cut out the tracing. Then unfold it and pin it to the felt.

3 Cut out two of these shapes in felt and pin them together.

← PUT FOLDED EDGE OF TRACING PAPER ON THIS LINE

4 Stitch round the edge of the felt leaving an opening between the flippers.

5 Pour the lentils or rice into the pliosaur and then sew up the hole.

SEW ON BUTTONS FOR EYES

Flying Reptiles

The flying reptiles are called pterosaurs. They lived at the same time as the dinosaurs. Some scientists think they were not reptiles, but were warm-blooded and furry.

The pterosaurs were not very strong fliers. Their wings were made of leathery skin supported by their fourth finger which had grown very long. They probably glided with outstretched wings and swooped down to catch fish or insects. If they were in danger, they could escape into the air, out of reach of the dinosaurs.

Dimorphodon lived about 190 million years ago and was one of the first pterosaurs. It measured nearly 2 m across its wings and had a long tail.

Like the other pterosaurs it had claws on its wings and large back claws. Its head was large and clumsy and it had sharp teeth in its beak-like jaws.

Toothless gliders

Pteranodon was one of the largest flying reptiles. It measured 8 m across its wings, but only weighed about 20 kg. Its claws were not very strong and it probably found it difficult to move on land.

It had a long, bony crest on the back of its head and a pointed beak with no teeth. It may have soared over the sea, looking for fish which it caught in its beak-like jaws and fed to its young.

Fossil pterosaur

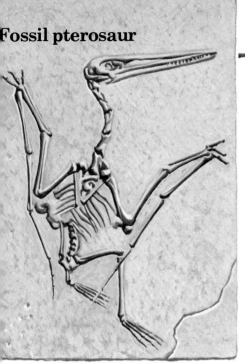

This is the fossil skeleton of *Pterodactylus*, one of the smallest pterosaurs. It shows the bones of the long fourth finger which supported the wing. You can see the teeth in its beak too. Its head was flat on top with not much space for the brain.

Pterodactylus was about the size of a starling. These pterosaurs lived together in flocks and probably slept hanging upside-down in trees or caves. They lived near the sea and ate insects, which they probably snapped up in their jaws as they flew.

New Discoveries

A fossil of the largest flying creature that has ever existed was found in 1975, in Texas, U.S.A. It was a pterosaur with a wing-span of about 12 m, which is larger than a two-seater aeroplane. This pterosaur has been named *Quetzalcoatlus*. It probably lived inland and fed on dead animals, like vultures do today.

Hairy pterosaur

Sometimes palaeontologists find fossils which change all their ideas about an animal. In 1966, in the U.S.S.R., they found the fossil of a pterosaur which looks as though it was covered with fluffy hair. It has been named *Sordes pilosus*.

Some scientists do not agree that the fossil shows hair. They think it may have been something like hair which kept the pterosaurs warm, or helped them to fly.

Rhamphorhynchus

Rhamphorhynchus measured about 2 m across the wings and had a long neck and head. Its tail ended in a diamond-shaped flap of skin which acted as a rudder and helped it to steer.

The bones of *Rhamphorhynchus* and other pterosaurs were hollow and filled with air. This made them light so they could glide more easily. Pterosaurs laid eggs but no nests have yet been found.

The First Bird

All the birds which live now are descended from the dinosaurs. The first bird is called *Archaeopteryx* and it lived 150 million years ago. *Archaeopteryx* developed from small dinosaurs like *Compsognathus*. Its skeleton was still like a reptile's but fossils show that it had feathers and so it was a true bird.

Archaeopteryx was about the size of a crow. It lived in woodlands and ate berries and insects. It could not fly very well and probably climbed trees and then glided down to the ground again.

Archaeopteryx had strong claws with one toe pointing backwards. This helped it to grip branches and perch in trees. Its long tail kept it steady as it flew down from the trees.

Feathered fossil

It probably found it difficult to take off from the ground as it was quite heavy. It climbed up trees, clinging to the bark with the long claws on its wings.

This fossil of *Archaeopteryx* shows the feathers on the wings and tail very clearly. It had teeth in its jaw like a reptile, and a long bony tail. Like modern birds, it had hollow bones to make it lighter. The name *Archaeopteryx* means "ancient wing".

Scaly head

Archaeopteryx's head was covered with scaly skin like the dinosaurs'. On the rest of its body the scales had become feathers.

The End of the Dinosaurs

About 65 million years ago, the dinosaurs became extinct. All the pterosaurs and the sea reptiles died out too. Palaeontologists do not know exactly why but they think perhaps these animals could not adapt to changes which were taking place on the Earth. When dinosaurs were alive the weather was warm all the year round. About 65 million years ago, it became cooler with cold winters. At the same time, great movements in the Earth crumpled the rocks and made high mountains.

Dinosaurs were cold-blooded and needed the sun to keep them warm. When their huge bodies got very cold it took too long for them to warm up again and many died.

There were probably other reasons too why dinosaurs died out. But now scientists have only the fossils in the rocks from which to find out why they became extinct.

The survivors

Great Tit

Mistle Thrush

Bullfinch

Tuatara lizards lived at the same time as the dinosaurs. But they did not become extinct. There are very few tuatara lizards living now and they may soon become extinct.

This is a mammal called *Protictis* which lived about 60 million years ago. Mammals are warm-blooded and they survived when the dinosaurs died out.

The birds that live today are the true descendants of the dinosaurs. They evolved from the first bird, *Archaeopteryx,* which developed from a small kind of dinosaur.

Living reptiles

Many different kinds of reptiles live today. Many of them are threatened with extinction because people kill them for their beautiful skins.

Tortoise

Snake

Lizard

Crocodile

Time Chart

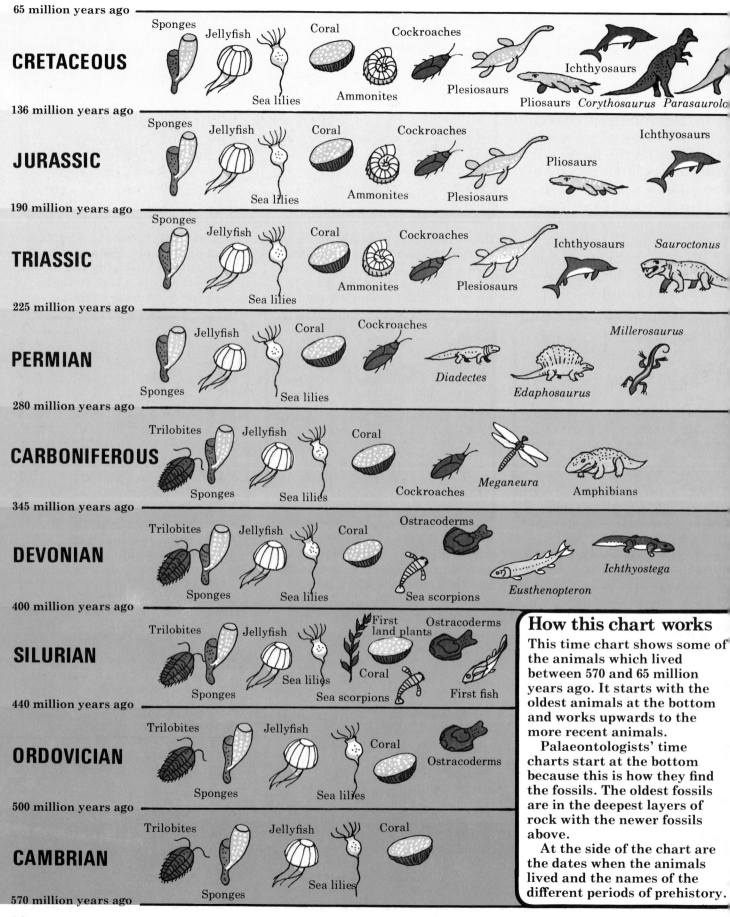

65 million years ago

CRETACEOUS

Sponges · Jellyfish · Coral · Cockroaches · Sea lilies · Ammonites · Plesiosaurs · Ichthyosaurs · Pliosaurs · *Corythosaurus* · *Parasaurolo*

136 million years ago

JURASSIC

Sponges · Jellyfish · Coral · Cockroaches · Ichthyosaurs · Sea lilies · Ammonites · Plesiosaurs · Pliosaurs

190 million years ago

TRIASSIC

Sponges · Jellyfish · Coral · Cockroaches · Ichthyosaurs · *Sauroctonus* · Sea lilies · Ammonites · Plesiosaurs

225 million years ago

PERMIAN

Jellyfish · Coral · Cockroaches · *Millerosaurus* · Sponges · Sea lilies · *Diadectes* · *Edaphosaurus*

280 million years ago

CARBONIFEROUS

Trilobites · Jellyfish · Coral · Sponges · Sea lilies · Cockroaches · *Meganeura* · Amphibians

345 million years ago

DEVONIAN

Trilobites · Jellyfish · Coral · Ostracoderms · Sponges · Sea lilies · Sea scorpions · *Eusthenopteron* · *Ichthyostega*

400 million years ago

SILURIAN

Trilobites · Jellyfish · First land plants · Ostracoderms · Sea lilies · Coral · Sponges · Sea scorpions · First fish

440 million years ago

ORDOVICIAN

Trilobites · Jellyfish · Coral · Ostracoderms · Sponges · Sea lilies

500 million years ago

CAMBRIAN

Trilobites · Jellyfish · Coral · Sponges · Sea lilies

570 million years ago

How this chart works

This time chart shows some of the animals which lived between 570 and 65 million years ago. It starts with the oldest animals at the bottom and works upwards to the more recent animals.

Palaeontologists' time charts start at the bottom because this is how they find the fossils. The oldest fossils are in the deepest layers of rock with the newer fossils above.

At the side of the chart are the dates when the animals lived and the names of the different periods of prehistory.

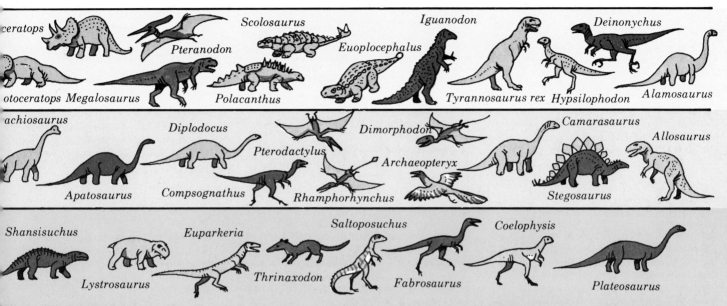

Triceratops Pteranodon Scolosaurus Euoplocephalus Iguanodon Deinonychus
Protoceratops Megalosaurus Polacanthus Tyrannosaurus rex Hypsilophodon Alamosaurus

Brachiosaurus Diplodocus Pterodactylus Dimorphodon Archaeopteryx Camarasaurus Allosaurus
Apatosaurus Compsognathus Rhamphorhynchus Stegosaurus

Shansisuchus Euparkeria Saltoposuchus Coelophysis
Lystrosaurus Thrinaxodon Fabrosaurus Plateosaurus

Prehistory Words

Ammonites
Sea creatures with coiled shells which lived 150 million years ago.

Amphibians
Animals, such as frogs, which live on land and lay their eggs in water.

Carnivores
Animals which eat meat.

Ceratopsians
Dinosaurs with horns and shields of bone round their necks.

Coprolite
Fossil animal dropping.

Dinosaurs
A group of reptiles which lived from 200 million to 65 million years ago.

Evolution
The way animals slowly change over a very long time and become different animals.

Fossils
Remains of ancient plants and animals preserved in the rocks.

Hadrosaurs
A group of dinosaurs, most of which had crests on their heads.

Herbivores
Animals which eat plants.

Ichthyosaurs
Swimming reptiles with fish-shaped bodies.

Invertebrates
Animals which do not have backbones.

Mammals
Animals which have fur, give birth to babies and can control their own body temperature.

Mammal-like reptiles
Reptiles which have some parts of their body like a mammal.

Ostracoderms
Fish-like sea creatures with thick, armoured skin which lived 400 million years ago.

Palaeontologist
A scientist who studies fossils to find out about prehistoric plants and animals.

Palaeontology
The study of prehistoric plants and animals.

Plesiosaurs
Reptiles with long necks which swim with four paddle-like legs.

Pliosaurs
Reptiles with short necks which swim with four paddle-like legs.

Pterosaurs
Flying reptiles with wings made of skin.

Reptiles
Animals which have scaly skin, lay eggs and cannot control their body temperature.

Sauropods
Very large, four-legged, herbivorous dinosaurs.

Sedimentary rock
Rock made from sand and mud which have been pressed down very hard and changed to rock.

Trilobites
Sea creatures with hard skin which lived 550 million years ago.

Vertebrates
Animals which have backbones.

Going Further

Finding fossils

If you find a fossil you could try and identify it using a book such as the *Hamlyn Guide to Minerals, Rocks and Fossils*. If you cannot find out what it is you could take it to your local museum, or send it to the Natural History Museum, Cromwell Road, London SW7 5BD, and ask them to help you. Remember to tell them where you found it and to pack it well.

Books to read

The Evolution and Ecology of the Dinosaurs by L. B. Halstead (Peter Lowe)
Prehistoric Animals by David Seymour (Black's picture information books, A. & C. Black)
Life before Man by Z. Spinar (Thames and Hudson)
A Closer Look at Prehistoric Reptiles by L. B. Halstead (Hamish Hamilton)

Museums

There is a large collection of fossils, including many fossil dinosaur skeletons, in the Natural History Museum, London. You can also see fossils in the Geology Museum, London.

In Australia, the National Museum of Victoria and the Australia Museum, Sydney have collections of prehistoric life.

Index

In this index, the English meanings of the Latin and Greek scientific names are in brackets. The names of individual plants and animals are written in *italics* and the names of groups of animals are in ordinary type.

Quiz answers

The reptiles in the Monster Quiz on page 15 are: 1. *Iguanodon*; 2. Pterosaurs; 3. *Stegosaurus*; 4. *Tyrannosaurus*; 5. *Brachiosaurus*; 6. Hadrosaurs.

The shadow monsters on page 23 are:
1. *Diplodocus*; 2. *Stegosaurus*;
3. *Compsognathus*; 4. *Protoceratops*;
5. *Tyrannosaurus rex*; 6. *Triceratops*;
7. *Rhamphorhynchus*; 8. *Iguanodon*;
9. *Polacanthus*; 10. *Scolosaurus*;
11. *Pteranodon*.